WALKING WITH JESUS IN SUFFERING

A 30-Day Lenten Journal

Friendship Press®

Friendship Press
P.O. Box 117
Wyncote, PA 19095

Library of Congress Catalog-in-Publication data available upon request

ISBN (hardcover): 978-1-961088-11-5

Verse selection and prompts by Heidi Hyland Mann
Cover and interior design by Laurie Ingram

Typesetting by Integra Software Services Pvt. Ltd.
Printed in the United States of America

About This Journal

Each *NRSVue Bible Journal* is offered with the hope that you will be inspired by your encounter with scripture and that journaling becomes a helpful part of your devotional journey.

The undated pages allow you to write at your own pace, with scripture passages and thoughtful writing prompts placed at regular intervals for you to meditate on, pray over, and write about as the Spirit moves you.

Lent is a time to reflect on Jesus's suffering. This reflective volume presents thirty key passages from the passion narratives and elsewhere to encourage you to reflect on Jesus's witness of hope in a suffering world.

date

ROMANS 8:18

I consider that the sufferings of this present time are not worth comparing with the glory about to be revealed to us.

date

"The sufferings of this present time" are very real. So how do you hold space both to honor them and to hope for better things to come?

date

ROMANS 8:22-23

The whole creation has been groaning together as it suffers together the pains of labor, and not only the creation, but we ourselves, who have the first fruits of the Spirit, groan inwardly while we wait.

date

Does knowledge that you don't suffer alone—that "the whole creation . . . suffers together"—help you wait for wholeness and healing?

date

date

date

ROMANS 8:24-25

Hope that is seen is not hope, for who hopes for what one already sees? But if we hope for what we do not see, we wait for it with patience.

date

Where do you find hope and patience amid suffering?

date

date

date

ROMANS 8:26

The Spirit helps us in our weakness, for we do not know how to pray as we ought, but that very Spirit intercedes with groanings too deep for words.

date

When you are hurting so much you can't even pray, does it help to know that other people—and even the Holy Spirit—are praying for you?

date

ISAIAH 40:29-31

[The LORD] gives power to the faint
 and strengthens the powerless.
. . . those who wait for the LORD shall renew their strength;
 they shall mount up with wings like eagles;
they shall run and not be weary;
 they shall walk and not faint.

date

Do you find discouragement or encouragement in the idea of waiting for the Lord when you feel weak and powerless?

date

date

date

MARK 14:32-34

They went to a place called Gethsemane, and [Jesus] said to his disciples, "Sit here while I pray." He took with him Peter and James and John and began to be distressed and agitated. And he said to them, "My soul is deeply grieved."

date

When have you felt distressed, agitated, deeply grieved? Does it help to know that Jesus, too, experienced these emotions?

date

date

date

MARK 14:35-36

And going a little farther, [Jesus] threw himself on the ground and prayed . . . , "Abba, Father, for you all things are possible; remove this cup from me, yet not what I want but what you want."

date

What forms of prayer have you found meaningful in times of trouble?

date

LUKE 22:43

[While Jesus prayed,] an angel from heaven appeared to him and gave him strength.

date

In what ways and through whom has God given you strength during struggles?

date

date

date

GALATIANS 6:2

Bear one another's burdens, and in this way you will fulfill the law of Christ.

date

How have you helped others who were burdened? Did you think of yourself as an instrument of Christ?

date

date

date

LUKE 22:47-48

Suddenly a crowd came, and the one called Judas, one of the twelve, was leading them. He approached Jesus to kiss him, but Jesus said to him, "Judas, is it with a kiss that you are betraying the Son of Man?"

date

If you've been betrayed by someone, what does it mean to you to know that Jesus experienced this too?

date

LUKE 22:49-51, 54

When those who were around him saw what was coming, they asked, "Lord, should we strike with the sword?" Then one of them struck the slave of the high priest and cut off his right ear. But Jesus said, "No more of this!" And he touched his ear and healed him. . . . Then they seized him and led him away, bringing him into the high priest's house.

date

Reflect on a time of fear or anger when you reacted with violence. What was the result?

date

date

date

JOHN 18:15-17

Simon Peter and another disciple followed Jesus. Since that disciple was known to the high priest, he . . . spoke to the woman who guarded the gate, and brought Peter in. The woman said to Peter, "You are not also one of this man's disciples, are you?" He said, "I am not."

date

Have you ever pretended not to know someone, for fear of how being associated with them might impact you?

date

date

date

LUKE 22:63-65

Now the men who were holding Jesus began to mock him and beat him; they also blindfolded him and kept asking him, "Prophesy! Who is it who struck you?" They kept heaping many other insults on him.

date

When you are insulted or mistreated, does it help to know that Jesus experienced such treatment? Why or why not?

date

PSALM 22:14-15 & PSALM 31:10

My heart is like wax;
it is melted within my breast;
my mouth is dried up like a potsherd,
and my tongue sticks to my jaws.

My strength fails because of my misery,
and my bones waste away.

date

When you are distressed or grieving, do you experience it in your body? If so, how?

date

date

date

LUKE 22:66-71

The assembly of the elders of the people . . . brought [Jesus] to their council. They said, "If you are the Messiah, tell us." He replied, "If I tell you, you will not believe, and if I question you, you will not answer. But from now on the Son of Man will be seated at the right hand of the power of God." All of them asked, "Are you, then, the Son of God?" He said to them, "You say that I am." Then they said, "What further testimony do we need? We have heard it ourselves from his own lips!"

date

What does it mean, in a society where many are treated unjustly by law enforcement and the courts, that Jesus also experienced this?

date

date

date

MARK 14:56-59

Many gave false testimony against [Jesus], and their testimony did not agree. Some stood up . . . , saying, "We heard him say, 'I will destroy this temple that is made with hands, and in three days I will build another, not made with hands.'" But even on this point their testimony did not agree.

date

Have you ever been falsely accused, whether of something large or small? How did it feel?

date

MATTHEW 26:15-17, 21, 26

Now at the festival the governor was accustomed to release a prisoner for the crowd, anyone whom they wanted. At that time they had a notorious prisoner called Jesus Barabbas. So after they had gathered, Pilate said to them, "Whom do you want me to release for you, Jesus Barabbas or Jesus who is called the Messiah?" And they said, "Barabbas." So he released Barabbas for them.

date

Have you ever wondered "Why me?" when you were suffering and someone else seemed to get off easy?

date

date

date

LUKE 23:23-25

[The chief priests] kept urgently demanding with loud shouts that [Jesus] should be crucified, and their voices prevailed. So Pilate gave his verdict that their demand should be granted . . . and he handed Jesus over as they wished.

date

What feelings does this reading evoke for you?

date

date

date

LUKE 23:26

As they led him away, they seized a man, Simon of Cyrene, who was coming from the country, and they laid the cross on him and made him carry it behind Jesus.

date

Think of a time you helped someone who was suffering, even if you didn't do so voluntarily. Did your feelings shift as you rendered aid?

date

LUKE 23:33, 39-43

When they came to the place that is called The Skull, they crucified Jesus there. . . . One of the criminals who were hanged there kept deriding him and saying, "Are you not the Messiah? Save yourself and us!" But the other rebuked him, saying, ". . . We indeed have been condemned justly, for we are getting what we deserve for our deeds, but this man has done nothing wrong." Then he said, "Jesus, remember me when you come in your kingdom." He replied, "Truly I tell you, today you will be with me in paradise."

date

When you are hurting, do you tend to lash out at others or empathize with others' pain?

date

date

date

MARK 15:33-34, 37

When it was noon, darkness came over the whole land until three in the afternoon. At three o'clock Jesus cried out with a loud voice . . . , "My God, my God, why have you forsaken me?" . . . Then Jesus gave a loud cry and breathed his last.

date

Have you ever felt abandoned by God? Did you find a way to express that? Reflect on what it means to you that even Jesus felt this way.

date

date

date

MATTHEW 27:57-60

When it was evening, there came a rich man from Arimathea named Joseph, who also was himself a disciple of Jesus. He went to Pilate and asked for the body of Jesus; then Pilate ordered it to be given to him. So Joseph took the body and wrapped it in a clean linen cloth and laid it in his new tomb, which he had hewn in the rock. He then rolled a great stone to the door of the tomb and went away.

date

Who has "gone over and above" for you when a loved one died or during another time of suffering?

date

ISAIAH 53:4

Surely he has borne our infirmities
and carried our diseases.

date

In what ways has God carried your sufferings or helped you bear them?

date

date

date

PSALM 31:21-22

Blessed be the Lord,
  for he has wondrously shown his steadfast love to me. . . .
I had said in my alarm,
  "I am driven far from your sight."
But you heard my supplications
  when I cried out to you for help.

date

When you have come through a time of suffering, do you sometimes see God's presence and activity in hindsight?

date

date

date

JOHN 20:19-20

When it was evening on that day, . . . and the doors were locked where the disciples were, . . . Jesus came and stood among them and said, “Peace be with you.” After he said this, he showed them his hands and his side. Then the disciples rejoiced when they saw the Lord.

date

Does it help you to know that the Risen Jesus still bore the marks of his suffering and death? What is the significance of scars?

date

PSALM 22:24 & 1 PETER 5:7

Be strong, and let your heart take courage,
all you who wait for the Lord.

Cast all your anxiety on [God], because he cares for you.

date

What counsel would you give someone who is suffering? How can we both hold space for another's suffering and offer hope?

date

date

date

2 CORINTHIANS 1:1-4

Blessed be . . . the God of all consolation, who consoles us in all our affliction, so that we may be able to console those who are in any affliction with the consolation with which we ourselves are consoled by God.

date

Does your suffering, and the comfort you've received, enable you in turn to support others in their suffering?

date

date

date

HEBREWS 13:5-6

[God] has said, “I will never leave you or forsake you.” So we can say with confidence,

“The Lord is my helper;
  I will not be afraid.”

date

What do these words of assurance mean to you?

date

REVELATION 21:4

[God] will wipe every tear from their eyes.
Death will be no more;
mourning and crying and pain will be no more,
for the first things have passed away.

date

How do you envision a world without suffering?

date

date

date

JOHN 14:27

[Jesus said,] "Peace I leave with you; my peace I give to you. I do not give to you as the world gives. Do not let your hearts be troubled, and do not let them be afraid."

date

In what specific ways does Jesus give you peace?

date

date

date